LIBERTY
Freedom not to sin

DAVID PAWSON

ANCHOR

Copyright © 2021 David Pawson Ministry CIO

The right of David Pawson to be identified as author of this
Work has been asserted by him in accordance with the
Copyright, Designs and Patents Act 1988.

First published in Great Britain in 2021 by
Anchor which is a trading name of David Pawson Publishing Ltd
Synegis House, 21 Crockhamwell Road,
Woodley, Reading RG5 3LE

No part of this publication may be reproduced or transmitted
in any form or by any means, electronic or mechanical,
including photocopy, recording or any information storage
and retrieval system, without prior permission
in writing from the publisher.

**For more of David Pawson's teaching,
including DVDs and CDs, go to
www.davidpawson.com**

**FOR FREE DOWNLOADS
www.davidpawson.org**

**For further information, email
info@davidpawsonministry.com**

ISBN 978-1-913472-44-3

Printed by Ingram Spark

This booklet is based on a talk. Originating as it does from the spoken word, its style will be found by many readers to be somewhat different from my usual written style. It is hoped that this will not detract from the substance of the biblical teaching found here.

As always, I ask the reader to compare everything I say or write with what is written in the Bible and, if at any point a conflict is found, always to rely upon the clear teaching of scripture.

David Pawson

PAUL'S LETTER TO THE GALATIANS HAS INFLUENCED CHURCH HISTORY

I don't know what your favourite book in the New Testament is, but mine is the last one I've studied. I get excited about the last one I've really been in to. Galatians I've found is nobody's favourite, but opinions about this little letter are very deeply divided, split right down the middle. People run hot or cold when they come to read Galatians. Here are some of the hot opinions: Luther said that Galatians was the best book in the Bible. He said this is *my* epistle, I am *married* to it; it is my Katie. Well now, if you know, he married a nun called Katherine who was his Katie. What he's saying is this is the book I'm married to. Another man said, this epistle was the pebble from the brook with which, like another David, Luther went forth to meet the Papal giant and smite him in the forehead. Quite a statement. You know that Goliath died of surprise, don't you? Such a thing had never entered his head before.

Well now, John Bunyan - John Bunyan, the author of Pilgrim's Progress - said 'I do prefer Luther's commentary on Galatians, except the Holy Bible, before all the books that I have ever seen as most fit for a wounded conscience'. That was John Bunyan's tribute to the old book, Martin Luther's Commentary on Galatians. That book had a profound effect on John Bunyan *and* on John Wesley. It was while somebody was reading from this that John Wesley felt his heart strangely warmed at quarter to nine on May 24th, 1738, in Aldersgate Street where there's now a Barclay's Bank, but there's a tablet on the wall to tell you that's where it happened.

So Galatians has had a profound influence on Christian history, and many Christians love this letter, but by no means all. Some dislike it intensely. It's been called a crucifixion epistle; it's been called a thorny jungle; been called explosive, every sentence a thunderbolt, so it's not a general favourite; why? I've written down five reasons.

GALATIANS IS EMOTIONAL

First, it's too emotional for some people. It is the most highly charged letter. It's written at white heat, it must have been written on asbestos papyrus or something because it really is a heated letter and some people don't like emotion in religion. Here's a classic story of a West Indian lady who went to a parish church in East London and she was used to joining in; and when the vicar preached, she said 'preach it brother, preach it brother, amen, hallelujah'. And finally, the verger came over and said, would you please be quiet you're disturbing the service. But, she said, I've got religion. And he said, you didn't get it here madam. Which I'm afraid was only too true, but you see for some reason, particularly in England, our public-school background has said, don't let emotion get into religion, keep it cool, keep it dignified. But when they read Galatians, here's a man who is writing at white heat, he is burning with something, absolutely burning and very angry - and people don't like that in religion.

GALATIANS IS PERSONAL

Some people say it's too personal a letter; far too much personality in it, it's too autobiographical and certainly Paul has put more about himself into this letter than any other. He talks about his physical handicaps at one point, pleads with them on the basis of his own weakness. But he's also mentioning at one point a public argument he had with no less than Peter where he had to stand up to Peter in front of a whole congregation, and say, Peter, you're wrong, so that even in the early church, the Apostles had their public differences. Thank God they had, they weren't like us today, too anxious to agree rather than differ, too anxious to avoid confrontation. No, when truth was at stake, even Peter and Paul would face each other up and fight for it.

GALATIANS IS INTELLECTUAL

Other people find it too intellectual a letter, and certainly it is very closely argued. Paul is really using all his Rabbinical background and training to argue the case he's making, and it's a very tight intellectual argument, and to tell you the truth, none of the translations that I've ever read really got to grips with the thread of argument, so I confess that I've actually translated it myself. It's been published but it's out of print unfortunately now. But I'll give you bits of it later because the argument is quite subtle and there are some very fine points in it and some people aren't bothered to use their intellect. You know, the greatest unexplored territory in the world is between your ears and we are to love God with all our *mind*. Let me confess the most frequent comment I get after preaching is a kind of mild rebuke that says, well you gave us something to think about today, and it's said in a tone of 'I didn't come to church to think'. Well I make no apologies for stretching your mind and Paul stretches your mind. It's a very tight argument and you need to study it very carefully and go through it again and again to see what he's saying.

GALATIANS IS SPIRITUAL

Some people find it too spiritual, surprisingly. I'm afraid it strips off all spiritual veneer, it really does hurt your pride this letter. If you've got any pride left, then don't read Galatians because you'll have none by the time you've finished. It really does go to the root of the matter and they just find it goes through beyond your mind and your heart, it goes through to the marrow, it's the sharp two-edged Word of God that penetrates.

GALATIANS IS CONTROVERSIAL

Above all, people have found it too controversial, too argumentative. Funny, but the modern mood is we don't want arguments in religion. We don't want to quarrel, let's just all be nice together - and Galatians is not that kind of a letter. Galatians argues *with other Christians* - not with unbelievers - it's arguing and it has caused many arguments. But if it hadn't caused that argument for Luther, the Reformation would not have occurred. So argument has benefitted us greatly and this is why it's not popular today because we don't like divisions, and differences lead to division and the two prime virtues considered today are *tolerance* and *tact* - and *neither* is a virtue in the Bible. But they are the two most considered Christian virtues in public opinion today - that we should be tolerant of one another and tactful in what we say. Well Jesus was neither, and his followers have been neither. They are controversialists, as he was. But we're afraid of discussing doctrine. Now, is this unwillingness to face our differences a good thing or a bad thing?

I was at a leaders' conference in January, 80 leaders, and, though they've met annually for many years, for the first time, they decided to spend a whole day discussing differences. And the organisers of the conference were really very tense thinking they'd have an explosion the following day and they spent the first day giving us all lectures on how Christians should handle differences. And I said to them, why are you so insecure? Do you think we can't differ and remain friends? I found I can have a better relationship with someone I can differ with and really hammer it out and be honest with one another, than the hypocrisy of papering over the cracks. But is it a good or a bad thing that we're unwilling for this? Well, it depends on whether the issues are primary or secondary. The trouble is we tend to get so heated over secondary issues that we are not really confronting people over primary things. I mean, does it really matter whether we have alcoholic wine or Ribena for Communion? And yet people get so upset about what's in the little cup on Sunday morning.

On the Sabbath issue, I don't believe that's an issue that Christians should be making too much of. Paul says, let each be fully persuaded in his own mind. If one wants to regard Sunday as special, that's his privilege. If another wants to regard every day as the Lord's day, that's their privilege. We haven't even the right to impose Sunday on each other as believers, never mind on unbelievers. And yet, Christians are making that a bit of a big issue. But when we come to Galatians, we're handling some of the biggest issues of all. And here, these are not secondary. You see, if you study Revelation, you'll be looking at the A-millennial, the pre-millennial and the post-millennial Christian viewpoints. And a friend of mine was asked when he arrived in the States - as soon as he got off the plane - Are you A-millennial, pre-millennial or post-millennial? He said, that is "a-pre-post-erous" question, which I thought was a neat answer. I wouldn't divide from other Christians on that issue.

PAUL DEALS WITH FUNDAMENTAL ISSUES AFFECTING THE GOSPEL

But on the things that Galatians is touching, I *would* divide over. These are fundamental issues without which you lose the Christian Gospel. So, I'm afraid it involves fighting and I want to tell you the biggest battles you will ever have are *inside* the church, and not outside. That is painful - because who likes a family that's arguing and yet it becomes necessary. You see, the Devil never destroyed the Church from the outside. Whenever he attacks the Church from the outside, the Church gets stronger and bigger. But he *can* destroy it from the inside and one of the quickest ways to do that is to pervert or corrupt or erode the Gospel - and if he can do that, he knows he's destroyed the Church from the inside. And I am afraid he is succeeding only too well in our day.

Now here we have two leading men, Peter and Paul, involved in a public confrontation on a fundamental issue. I want to say a little thing here that may not be popular about gender. I believe God has given the responsibility of fighting for and protecting the doctrine of the Church to the men - and it is a tragedy that we don't have more strong men of conviction who will fight to protect the Gospel. There are many women who *want* to and who *try* to, but I believe - and I'm confessing a weakness of my gender now - there are not enough men prepared to stick their neck out and confront error when they hear it or see it. Well I just throw that in. But Peter and Paul did fight it out. Peter *was* in the wrong and Paul *was* in the right, and the Bible has been honest enough to share that with us, and clearly God wanted us to know about that confrontation.

Now let's look at the letter. A letter in the ancient world - there were many - is nevertheless a unique form of writing because in those days with no public mail service, letters were neither cheap nor easy to send. You had to find someone who was going to a place and you then paid them to go. That letter was carried by hand. Well if a letter cost *you* £50 a time, you would not write so many. There was no such thing as holiday postcards from Pompeii then. And so letters were very important, much more important than they are today. We just scribble off notes all the time, but they only wrote when there was something *very, very important* to say because it would cost so much to send, and be so difficult to get through. So they had to have a very good reason for sending one.

The form in which they wrote of course was just a long strip of parchment rolled up. And they had a very sensible habit - I don't know why we don't do the same - when you began to unroll it, the first thing you saw was the name of the sender, and then the address to which it was sent, and the readers, the recipient. Now you see what we do is we send a whole letter, and I get many letters, pages long - some people want to tell me their life history - and they always put the name of the sender at the end. So you find yourself opening a letter and then looking on the last page to find out who sent it. What a silly habit, isn't it? Why don't we say it at the beginning, this is from me. And that's what they used to do so that as you unrolled it, you got... well, the postman just had to unroll the first inch or two to know where to take it, and who to give it to, and the person who read it knew immediately.

And then another custom was that, as soon as you did that, you wrote the greetings. You always greeted them in some way, and then it was almost an unwritten rule you said something nice about the person you sent it to, *especially* if you were going to say something not so nice later. Now it's interesting that Paul follows this form of a letter *almost* every time, and he begins that way even with the Corinthians and, boy, they were in trouble. They were getting drunk at the Lord's Supper. They didn't believe in the resurrection anymore; they were dividing into cliques. They were doing nothing but tongues when they got into worship. It was a real mess, but he begins the letter, "I thank God that you've got every spiritual gift." It begins with something nice before it says something nasty, that's the custom. And that makes it all the more unusual that when he writes to the Galatians, he has *nothing* nice to say. He would have done so if he could, but this letter, no compliments, no I thank God for you, nothing. He's just straight in with a red hot criticism, because there's something he's just so filled with, he's exploding with it, and he can't even wait to follow the usual courtesies.

Now one other thing of general introduction to letters, to epistles. When you read an epistle, you must remember you're only hearing *one side* of a conversation. A correspondence *corresponds* to a situation, and therefore you have to read *between the lines* as well as the lines. It's rather like, have you ever been in a room where the telephone rings and somebody else has answered the 'phone and you've only heard their side of the conversation? I'll guarantee you try and construct the other side, don't you? Well, let me just try that and see if you can put together the situation that I'm speaking to on the 'phone.

> Hello.
>
> It's arrived then.
>
> Congratulations.
>
> Yesterday.
>
> How much does it weigh?
>
> What colour is it?
>
> They usually are.

LIBERTY - FREEDOM NOT TO SIN

Do you think you'll have enough use for it?

Mind you, they can be quite dangerous.
But then it's fairly flat in your part of the world.

I think you'll find it a bit thirsty.

Is it the petrol or the diesel version?

Alright. Ultimately, I'm 'phoning a farmer who's just won a tractor in a sweepstake. Now at what stage did you even begin to think that way? Do you see what I mean? When you only hear one side of a conversation, your brain can get the wrong idea about the other side of it if you're not careful, because you come to it with preconceived notions. Now when you read an epistle, somehow you have to try and reconstruct the situation to which it's written, and you read between the lines. You say, 'What was happening that needed this letter?' and it's a most healthy way of studying the letters. You don't need to study a gospel that way, but you *do* need to study a letter that way. Well, we're going to use that method now to look at Galatians.

WRITER: PAUL (The apostle)
READERS: CHURCHES in GALATIA (north or south?)
OCCASION: 1. ADDITIONS to the MESSAGE
ISSUE: 2. ATTACKS on the MESSENGER
    a. CIRCUMCISION?
    b. JUDAISM?
    c. SALVATION!
        i. WORKS ALONE
        ii. WORKS PLUS FAITH.
        iii. FAITH PLUS WORKS.
        iv. FAITH ALONE.

WHY WAS THIS LETTER WRITTEN?

Why was it written? What questions was it answering, what problems was it giving the solution to? That's how you study every letter in the New Testament. Well now, the writer of the letter – there's no doubt about who this was, Paul; no debate whatever. And it is probably the first letter he ever wrote to a church or to churches and that's why I take it first, before Romans. Romans was one of the last letters he wrote, though it comes first in your Bible. So I just reverse the order. This was one of the earliest, probably *the* first that he ever wrote. By any standard, Paul was one of the greatest men who ever lived. Born in Tarsus in southern Turkey, as we know it now. Tarsus had the third most important university. After Athens number 1 and Alexandria number 2, Tarsus was number 3 in academic importance. It was a bit like Durham to Oxford and Cambridge, or am I offending someone? He had Jewish parents, who were Roman citizens and spoke the Greek language. Now what a background.

You know, God prepares us for ministry even before we're born. But he prepares us with our experiences long before we know him. He's putting things into us that he can use later. What a mixed background, a really Jewish Jew, whose parents were Roman citizens and therefore *he* became one - he inherited that status - *and* spoke the Greek language. He was taught a trade, as every good Jewish man is. Every Jewish man must learn to work with his hands. That's a healthy thing. You see, in Greek society, if you worked with your hands, you were lower down the social scale than those who worked with their heads and were pen pushers and we have inherited that attitude. But in the Bible a tent maker and a fisherman - that's something else. Paul says, in one of his letters to Thessalonica, you should all work with your hands, all of you. I've given you an example to do that. The dignity of manual labour. Jesus was a carpenter for 18 years.

So Paul was a tent maker, probably for the army, and then he studied in Jerusalem University under Professor Gamaliel and he became an ultra-orthodox, fanatical proud "Hebrew of the Hebrews, Pharisee of the Pharisees." You couldn't get anybody more Jewish than Saul of Tarsus. A Judaistic bigot. And he really tried very hard to keep every law of Moses, 613 of them. We try and make do with ten, but actually there were 613. If you're going to keep the Law, keep the lot. Don't just choose ten, keep them all - and he did. He does admit that he had real problems with one. It was very interesting which one, it was the tenth commandment - don't be greedy, don't covet. And it's interesting that that's the one commandment that deals with your inner motivation. The others deal with outward behaviour, but that deals with the heart. And he said he had real problems with that one, but he managed to keep the lot – "as touching the Law, blameless." Now there are not many who could say that. And he had achieved a great deal of self-righteousness.

He attacked everybody who attacked Judaism. If anybody undermined the Judaistic faith he went for them. He was an anti-missionary in that sense, and especially these new followers of Jesus, claiming that he was God, that was so against Jewish monotheism, "Hear, O Israel, the Lord our God is *one*." How can there be another, and he felt this was the ultimate blasphemy and he was determined to wipe it out. And in fact, he set out to destroy this new faith and he watched Stephen stoned to death. That was it. From then on, he began to be pricked in his conscience. It was hard for him to "kick against the pricks." And he saw that young man die, and that young man, as he died, said, "I can see Jesus on the right hand of God; into your hands I commit my spirit." And that made him fight this new faith even harder, because now he was fighting himself and there's nobody who fights so hard as people who are fighting their own conscience. Then on the Damascus road, he met Jesus.

Do you know that all a Jew needs to become a believer in Jesus is to know that he's alive? I was once preaching near Cambridge and a Jewess was in the congregation and afterwards she came to me. She said, are you trying to tell me that Jesus of Nazareth is still alive? I said, that's what I'm saying. She said, but if he is then he must be *our* Messiah - I like the little word *our*, you know. She meant hers, not mine. And I said, that's right; she said, how could I find out if he's alive? I said, just try talking to him right there. She found out. And do you know within ten minutes, she was teaching me the Bible. She said, then this, and this, and this, and she'd got it all. The one thing she hadn't got was the knowledge that Jesus of Nazareth was still around, and that's all the Jewish nation will need – "they will look on him whom they pierced", and a nation will be born in a day. I can see that happening; and Saul was a forerunner of all that happening to the rest of his people on the Damascus road and he became the Gentile missionary. And even on that first day, the Lord said, I'm going to send you to the Gentiles.

Well now, that's the man who wrote this letter and he became the most enthusiastic follower of Jesus ever, an ardent propagator of the faith he once tried to destroy. And so he knew both Judaism and Christianity inside out. And he'd switched from one to the other. That's the background; and on successive missionary journeys he planted churches throughout the then known world, constantly pioneering fresh territory. He called it 'colonising for Christ', a lovely phrase.

WHO WAS IT WRITTEN TO?

Now what about the readers? There's a bit of a problem here because there are two Galatia's - and scholars waste a lot of ink arguing which it was. In what we now call Turkey, there was a group of cities in the north called North Galatia, there was a group of cities in the south called South Galatia and the whole thing is, was it written to the North Galatians or the South? We have a little interest in the north because that was Celtic, it was originally colonised by Gauls - people from Gaul - and later, about the year 250 BC they would send mercenaries, hired soldiers, all over Europe, and those soldiers became the Irish, the Scots and the Welsh - the Celtics - and so there are Scots, Irish and Welsh who would love to believe this letter was written to them, but I have to disappoint them all - I don't believe it was written to North Galatia. South Galatia was a group of cities - Lystra, Derby, Antioch, Iconium - and these were the towns to which Paul had already gone. It's understandable that you would write a letter like this because when Paul had planted churches, as soon as he had elders in them he left, and he left them entrusted to these new elders and to the Head of the Church in heaven and his Vicar on earth, the Holy Spirit, and he trusted them and the Holy Spirit to continue.

Unfortunately, what happened to them has happened to many new fellowships today. Other men come in and try and take over the work. Always beware of men who come and take over, they are often dangerous men, and in fact there are men looking around building their empires by taking into themselves fellowships that other people have planted, that are not their work, but getting them under their wing. It's dying down a bit now in Britain but some years ago it was happening all over the place. And it's so often later leaders who come in and take over the work who take it astray, and lead it down the wrong paths, and Paul had that. And I'm afraid the people who did it were Jewish believers, who followed Paul around everywhere. They were his biggest problem and they said to the Gentiles, don't listen to Paul, he's only given you half the story. He's brought you to faith yes, but he didn't bring you fully into the faith because you need the Law of Moses as well as Christ.

OLD TESTAMENT LAWS

I'm amazed how often I go into churches in this country and see the ten commandments stuck up on the wall. I'll tell you something about one of the first churches I became pastor of in 1952. The first church in *England* that I became pastor of - I was a pastor in Shetland Islands before that - but the first church in England had the ten commandments up on the wall behind my head in the pulpit in chocolate brown gothic lettering and I said, the first thing I'm going to do is paint that out and I got a pot of paint and I just painted all over it. And do you know, there was an outcry; somebody said, there's nothing to read during the sermon now. I said, well you can play bingo with the hymn board numbers but I'm not preaching in front of that, I really am not because that's not what I've come to preach. Well, they said, we've got to have something there, so I did put up a cross in those days and put that up on the wall. But I'd rather preach that than the ten commandments.

We'll come back to that in a moment; I may be shocking you. But you see, everywhere Paul went and brought them the full Gospel of Christ, these *believers* - Jewish believers - followed up and said, of course he hasn't told you everything and we've now come to give you the whole situation. That's exactly how leaders talk today, when they try and take over other people's fellowships. Well, good as far as you've gone but we've got more and we've got the whole thing for you - and they walk in and take over other people's work.

Now South Galatia, I'm sure it's south, had those key cities which Paul had established the work in, gone back and appointed Elders, left them with the Holy Spirit to guide them, but then these other leaders came along and spoiled the work. Now, Paul has heard some very bad news about his baby churches, the ones that *he* laboured to bring into being. His work was being undone and two things were happening. First of all, they were making *additions* to his message, it was the Gospel *plus* - and that again is something we've got to watch. So many sects and cults around *add* to the Gospel and they usually add another book to the Bible, have you noticed? They add Mary Baker Eddy's Science and Health to the Bible, or they add Joseph Smith's book to the Bible. Beware of anybody who says, you've got to have this book as well as your Bible. It's the Gospel plus again, something is being *added on* and you can only put so much luggage in a canoe before it overturns. Or to put it another way, rot starts in the pulpit, dry rot.

BEWARE BAD TEACHING

Bad teaching is *the* one thing we've got to be on our guard against - bad teaching. But when you add to the Gospel, you invariably attack the messenger who brought the original Gospel, and it wasn't just that these teachers were *adding* to Paul's Gospel, they were attacking the messenger, and indeed that's one way if you don't like what a man says, you attack *him*, you see? You say things about *him*, and unfortunately, they were attacking the messenger as well as adding to the message, that's what was happening.

So let's look at what the issue actually was. What was all the trouble about? Well a first reading of the letter and you would think it was about circumcision, that seems to be the thing that Paul is going for hard. Well let's look at circumcision. Was he making a mountain out of a mole-hill? Why get so hot up about this little thing? If people want to be circumcised that's okay. Was he justified in making such a song and dance about this Jewish custom of circumcision.? A minor operation, the removal of part of the reproductive organ of the male, not practised on the females in Judaism, though it is in certain tribes in Africa. It's now done for medical or social reasons. It's a widespread habit in the Semitic world, largely for hygienic reasons in that climate; but to the Jews, it had a religious significance. To the Jew it was fundamental. There was a day when Hitler's gestapo would just line up people in the streets of Berlin and make them drop their trousers to find out who they should cart off to the concentration camp. It was the mark of a Jew and of course, it was only on males because in the Jewish world it is the male who inherits and the inheritance passes down, the promises pass down, through the male line. Therefore females were not circumcised, and it was a sign of eligibility to inherit the blessing promised to Abraham. And it was even said by God to Abraham that if any Jewish male was not circumcised, he had to be thrown out of the people of God because he'd broken the covenant. Part of the covenant with Abraham was that every male descendant would bear this mark, so that to a Jew, this means everything.

Three things that mean everything to the Jew are the Passover, the Sabbath and circumcision. Whatever else they do or do not do - they may be liberal Jews, or non-practising Jews - but those three things still apply. Probably Kosher food is the fourth that most would observe, but not all. But those three things - circumcision, the Sabbath and the Passover, those are an absolute must. Paul argues in Galatians that the promise made to Abraham was only intended for one male descendant of Abraham, that the word *seed* in scripture was singular, not plural - and that when God said "to Abraham and his seed", he didn't mean to all his male descendants but to one of them. And Paul argues that when that one male seed came, which was Jesus, then circumcision becomes obsolete because now it's been inherited. The one to whom it was promised has got it so there's no point in circumcising anybody. Do you follow the argument? And you'll find that in Galatians 3.

So it was a sign of inheritance. Jesus had that sign, Jesus was circumcised, and he was the one who inherited. Paul had been circumcised as a Jewish male in his Jewish day and he did actually circumcise Timothy, and Timothy came from Galatia, and yet Paul circumcised him. Why? Because he was going to accompany Paul in his missionary work and Paul always went into the synagogue first and preached to Jews and Timothy would never have managed to get in with him if he hadn't been circumcised. So Paul did it purely as an act of accommodation for evangelism. In the same way that C.T. Studd and others grew pigtails when they went to China to try and open a door, to get alongside people. But here is Paul who would circumcise Timothy from Galatia for that reason, who is now saying how *dare* you consider it? And some people said, Paul you're inconsistent, you've circumcised Timothy, why shouldn't we? So that's the occasion, that's the situation.

But behind circumcision lies something else. His language by the way reminds one again that the Bible is not a book for children, it's a book for adults. The tragedy is that most people stop reading it when they become adult, but it's not a children's book. But Paul really uses the strongest language. He says, I just wish those who would cut off your foreskins would go the whole hog and castrate themselves. Then they wouldn't be able to reproduce themselves. Strong language. Why is he saying this? At one point he says, if you have your foreskin cut off you will have Christ cut off from you. Now very blunt, strong language, quite unlike some of his other letters. Why is he saying this? Why is he so against circumcision? The answer is because behind circumcision lay Judaism. And

LIBERTY - FREEDOM NOT TO SIN

Judaism is, I am afraid, still a religion of works, it's a religion of saving yourself by keeping the commandments. It's an impossible task, but so many people try it. And the danger of putting the ten commandments up on the wall is precisely that you're communicating to people you've got to live this way in order to get right with God, and an outsider coming in is faced straightaway with "Thou shalt".

By the way, it's being said of some liberal scholars these days that they take the word 'not' out of the ten commandments and put it into the creed, so that now the ten commandments are 'thou shalt commit adultery and thou shalt steal and thou shalt do all the other things' and the creed says I do *not* believe in the virgin birth and I do *not* believe in the bodily resurrection. That's a rather neat criticism, but faced with all 'thou shalt nots', apart from anything else, it gives the impression that we're against everything, that we're negative and that if you come anywhere near God, he'll stop you having fun. You know, that God is a 'thou shalt not-er' and that he faces you straightaway with the things you mustn't do. That's a tragic negative impression that's given.

Now Christianity is rooted in Judaism, which in turn is rooted in the Old Testament, as *we* are. But how much of the former should be kept in the latter? How much of the Old Testament comes through to the New? How many of those 613 laws actually apply to us? That's one of the biggest questions you've got to face when you study the Old and the New Testaments. Let me give you an example. I cannot ever tell Christians to tithe because it's an old covenant law and it belongs to the law of Moses, it's *never* mentioned in the New Testament, when speaking to Gentile believers. Jews did it, but no Gentile believer was ever told to tithe. We *are* told to give, and I listened to a young man preaching on tithing and he'd used his computer or his concordance and he typed in tithing and got all the print outs and he actually said this, and he was honest enough to say this; he said, there are blessings attached to tithing, and he gave us them all, for example "prove me now herewith if I don't open the windows of heaven and pour out a blessing on you", and then he said but there are curses attached to tithing as well, which is true. And he proceeded to tell us about a curse in the Old Testament - which is there - that our grandchildren and great-grandchildren will suffer if *we* do not bring our tithes. I looked at the faces of the congregation and boy, the fear of causing their great-grandchildren to suffer, and it's no wonder the offering was pretty big the following Sunday. But I was horrified; I said, that's wicked. In the New Testament, it's on altogether a different principle. "The Lord loves a *cheerful giver*," which doesn't mean grin and bear it, it means that you *want to give*, that's what he's after now, not people forced to give in case their great-grandchildren suffer. That belongs to the old covenant. I hope I have made it clear.

Sabbath law is another one. Now we've really got to think what we're doing before we apply old covenant laws to Christians, because if you apply *some* of them you must apply *all* of them, and if you apply the *blessing* you must apply the *curse*. Now, are we prepared to do that? I'm not. You see, I believe we've got to rethink this issue; and Paul is saying, if you get circumcised, that's just the camel's nose in the tent and you will soon have the hump and all. If you go the way of circumcision for the reason these teachers are teaching it, then *all* the other 613 laws will follow and come in. That's why he is so anxious - not about circumcision itself, but it *opened the door* to Judaism, and he was finished with that. He'd tried it, he'd done his best at it and it left him. In fact he said, when I consider the commandments I've *kept*, not the ones I've broken, but the commandments I kept, he said, I feel like a little boy holding up his potty and saying look what I've done. And he uses a very crude word in Greek for dung. "I count it but dung". There's a good Anglo-Saxon equivalent, he said that's what it is, my self-righteousness; that's all it produced, and he said, thank God I'm delivered from all that, set free from it. You see, I think if you tell people to keep the laws of Moses, you're consigning them to hell because they can't do it.

Just by way of light relief, let me tell you about an experience. I had a telephone call from Israel; all the Christian churches - Arab and Jewish and missionary - from Israel were getting together in Tiberius in Galilee for a conference and they'd really come to a point of disagreement and they wanted someone from outside to come and help them sort it out. And they rang me up and said, would you catch the next plane to Israel and come and help us with this problem? Well I said, I'll try, but when I found out the cost of a last-minute seat, it was about £830 return and I hadn't got it and I didn't feel I could ask them for so much. So I thought, what can I do? There was a group of Arab and Israeli young people out there praying for me to come, and they asked the Lord how much he could get me out for, and the Lord told them in shekels, £120, and those young people collected £120.

I went to Luton airport and I said, have you got a charter plane going to Jerusalem, could you put me on a charter plane? They said, we've got one going today but it's full and they said, would you mind a crew seat? And I said, not at all; and it was one of those backward facing upright seats. I had a bad back for days, but I was sitting facing backwards and I looked around and I thought, I'm the only Gentile on this plane. I was facing four Rabbis. So we had a Kosher meal and then I thought, it's time we started talking. So I said to the first one, excuse me, but do you keep the law of Moses? He said, of course. I said what about this one? Oh well, he said no, the Chief Rabbi allows us to do something different instead of that now. Oh, I said, you don't keep that one now? No, he said, no. So I said to the second, do you keep the law of Moses? Of course. I said, what about this one? Well, he said, you see we haven't got a temple now so we can't have a sacrifice, we can't do that one now. Oh you don't keep that one? I went right along and finally the fourth one, he said, what are you, orthodox or liberal? So I said, neither. We went on a bit, and I'll never forget. One of them, the second one, said straight off, I know what you are, you're a Christian and he said, and you believe Jesus died to save you from all this. I said, bull's eye, spot on. He said, so you think you don't need to keep all these up? I said, I could no more keep them than you can.

We had a great conversation and we finally landed at Ben Gurion airport, only too quickly. But you see, you can't keep them all, it's an impossible task. Don't put people under the law, put them under grace. Now that is very, very important. There is a law we're under, but it's the law of Christ, it's not the Law of Moses, that Law's obsolete, it's been done away.

But you know one of the biggest problems in the church today, and that's why Galatians is so relevant, we're constantly giving people a *mixture* of the law of Christ and the Law of Moses, constantly getting mixed up. Why do you think churches today have vestments and altars and incense, and priests? We don't need *any* of those things, they belong to the Law of Moses, but they've crept back in. When are we going to be bold enough to apply Galatians as it was meant to be applied?

IS SALVATION BY WORKS, FAITH OR A MIXTURE?

Throughout the book of Acts, we see a loosening of the ties between Judaism and Christianity. Stephen began it and his martyrdom - well he was the first martyr for this particular issue. And Phillip, baptising the Ethiopian eunuch, took it a little further and then Peter with Cornelius, and soon the

LIBERTY - FREEDOM NOT TO SIN

Jewish believers in Jerusalem were very, very suspicious about this new faith being taken to Gentiles. It didn't seem Jewish enough for them, and so finally Paul went up to Jerusalem to challenge the very heart of the church that was sending out these anti-missionaries as it were, who were saying it's not just enough to believe, you've got to be circumcised as well.

And the real issue was not circumcision - behind that lay the question: Should a Gentile become a Jew when they become a Christian? The question of Judaism as such, but behind that was the big issue and the real issue was *salvation* itself. *Not* Judaism or circumcision, but *salvation*, and the whole question was: Is it by works or by faith or a mixture? Now most religions of the world are salvation by works - you must pray, you must fast, you must give alms and so on, and then at the end of it all you'll get right with God, you save yourself by your own efforts. And do-it-yourself religion does appeal to people because it leaves them with their pride - I achieved it. It is *self*-righteousness and God *hates* self-righteousness. He would rather deal with sin than self-righteousness. Jesus just couldn't get on with self-righteous people. He was a friend of sinners but the *self*-righteous, the Pharisees, he couldn't get on with at all. Is salvation by works alone? Do you really have to do your best and really work hard to get there? Or is salvation works plus faith? That's very common.

I was a Chaplain in the Royal Air Force and I was the OD Chaplain, the Odd-Bod, the Other Denominations. There was an RC and a C of E and when a new bunch of men arrived, the C of E would say, how many of you have been christened C of E? And he'd walk off with 70%, then the RC would take off everybody with an Irish accent - and I would be left. I was left with Baptists, Methodists, Salvationists, Buddhists, Hindus, Muslims, Agnostics, Atheists. It's fascinating to be Chaplain to Atheists you know. That's another story. But when the men were seated before me, I used to say, how many Methodists, and how many Baptists, how many Salvationists, put their hands up. And in the same tone of voice, I'd say, and how many Christians? Dead silence. Occasionally, a lad would put his hand up and smile, but usually they would look around to see if anybody else was. I said, come on, you told me how many Methodists and Baptists, well how many Christians? And they used to say, but what do you mean by Christian, Padre? And I'd say, well, what do you think I mean? And they always said the same thing - someone who keeps the ten commandments. Now I guess they picked that up in church as children, reading them on the wall, but I said, Okay, I'll accept that, a Christian is someone who keeps the ten commandments. How many Christians are there here? And again, there'd be real uncertainty, and then somebody would say, but Padre you can't keep them all; and I would say, well, how many do you have to keep to be a Christian? They always said, six out of ten. I said, Okay I accept that, a Christian is someone who keeps six out of ten commandments. How many Christians are there here? And it led to a tremendous discussion of what a Christian is. And I made *them* do the discussion and this was what they were really struggling with. You see, works plus faith says, do as many as you can and then have faith for what you don't manage. Keep as many commandments as you can, and then ask God to forgive what you didn't manage to keep. That is the most common understanding of Christianity that there is in our country: The do-gooding.

"FAITH FROM FIRST TO LAST"

Then there are those who say, no it's faith plus works. You start with faith, and then you go on to works and you keep the Law *after* you've believed, but you've got to keep the Law. You see, that's what the Judaisers were saying, start with faith and then keep the Law. And that's why Paul was going to say to the Galatians: "Having started in the Spirit, are you going to continue in the flesh?" Because Law belongs to flesh. That's your effort, it's not the Spirit doing it in you, it's *you* doing it. And what Paul was fighting for was faith alone – "faith from first to last" as he often puts it, faith from beginning to end. He said, "I'm not ashamed of the Gospel; it's the power of God that saves everyone who *goes on believing"* - there's that continuous present tense which is in the original Greek of the New Testament. For it is "from faith to faith", "faith from first to last" as the NIV puts it. In other words, we cannot compromise on this, you *go on believing*. That's the heart of it. You don't believe at the beginning and then work for it. You go on believing - and there's a big difference between telling people they need to go on believing and telling them they need to keep the Law now, a huge difference.

So this is the real issue that Paul is fighting. What he is fighting for is Christian freedom. To introduce the Law at any stage is to put them under a curse. Because the only pass-mark that Jesus will accept for the Law is 100%, you either keep them *all* or you've broken the Law, and that's true with the traffic laws. If I'm stopped by a speed cop I can't say, but officer I stopped at every red light on the way here. He says, I don't care if you stopped at *every* red light, you have broken the law. And that's what God says, because the Law is not just a string of pearls, it's a necklace, holiness is a complete thing. If you break it at any point, the pearls all fall on the ground. You've broken the Law, it doesn't matter if you've broken one or nine or ten.

It's like three people stranded on a rock with the incoming tide and there's a three metre deep bit of sea now between the rock and the sand and the first man jumped and he only managed to jump a third of the way and he drowned. The second man was a better jumper and he managed two-thirds of the way and he drowned. The third man only missed by six inches, but he was lost too.

WHY DID GOD GIVE THE LAW?

And actually, keeping the Law, it doesn't matter whether you managed a bit or a lot - if you didn't make it 100%, you're just as lost as if you broke most of them. That's how God thinks, that's what his Word says. "Cursed be he who does not continue in all these Laws to go on doing them", says the scripture. Now that's the curse you're under if you try and keep the commandments and get to heaven under your own steam. But the Gospel has a different way of righteousness altogether. Then of course the obvious question is: Then why did God give the ten commandments, why did he give the Law of Moses at all? And the answer is in Galatians, and the answer is: It is by the straight edge of the Law that we realise how crooked we are. In other words, it's only the Law that tells you you're a sinner; you don't find out how wrong you've been until you study the Law of God, then you discover. It was introduced to prepare us for Christ by showing us that we couldn't keep that Law, and that's why preaching the ten commandments can bring a person to conviction of sin because they know there's no way they can keep it, especially the way Jesus reinterpreted those Laws.

LIBERTY, LEGALISM, LICENSE

So we come to the real matter of liberty. Now we've got an accompanying picture, a visual aid.

LIBERTY - FREEDOM NOT TO SIN

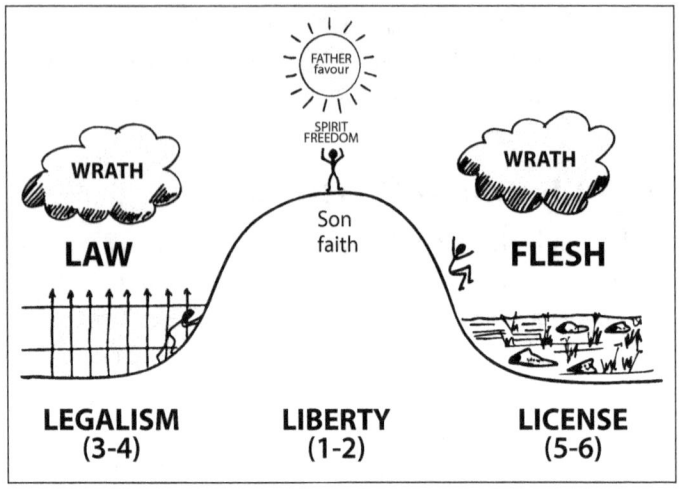

That's the whole of Galatians in one picture, a very simple picture but I need to explain it. Where shall we start? The three things that we're talking about are Legalism, Liberty and License. And legalism is an enemy of liberty but what people don't always realise is that license is too. And chapters 1 to 2 of Galatians talk about our liberty in Christ - under the favour of the Father, we're in the sunshine of his love in the freedom of the Spirit - and the foundation is faith in the Son. So Father, Son and Spirit are giving us the freedom of standing up on the mountain top.

But there are two ways of losing that freedom. One is to slip back into Law, which is a cage – we're trapped in it - we try and climb out but we can't. You once get back under Law and you're in bondage, in slavery, and, as the illustration shows, you're under the wrath of God again because you can't keep it. But there's another way to lose your liberty and that's to slip down the other side into the swamp of the flesh and that also is bondage, but it's bondage to yourself. One way, you'll invariably become in bondage to others because of their rules and regulations; the other way, you become in bondage to your own desires, and you're under the wrath of God again. And you've lost your freedom.

STRIDING EDGE, LAKE DISTRICT, UK

Have any of you ever been to Striding Edge on Helvellyn in the Lake District? That's a perfect illustration because it's a very sharp path right along a high ridge and either side are two huge hollows, we call them corries. They've been hollowed out by great balls of ice in the ice age revolving, and as the two balls revolve, they leave this very sharp ridge. The Matterhorn in Switzerland was the result of three balls of ice revolving, and it leaves a three-pointed thing, but the two-sided ridge is the result of two balls of ice. And it's wonderful to walk along the Striding Edge but my, if you do it in a high wind, the only safe way to do it is on your knees. There's a moral there. Alright. Preaching again.

Well Striding Edge - you see, it is a delicate striding edge that we walk in the liberty of the Spirit. It's so easy to slip one way or the other; and I would say the biggest danger to Christians in their liberty is legalism, surprisingly. Because license is pretty obvious. It's when churches start

LIBERTY - FREEDOM NOT TO SIN

making extra rules and regulations that you get so easily into legalism, and legalism kills the Spirit dead. You go into a legalistic fellowship and you can tell it straight away, everybody has pursed lips, you know? Have you seen that? And there's a kind of set expression, a *hard* expression on people's faces; they've got under the Law again. They're keeping it, but oh, it makes you tough, it makes you hard. It's not the liberty of the Spirit. Legalism makes the whole thing a matter of rules rather than relationships, that's probably the key, and a person thinks they're a Christian because they're keeping the rules: Don't smoke, don't gamble, don't drink, don't do this, don't do that, and so they're keeping the rules, but the relationship has gone.

Just to give you a homely illustration of this. There was a young man came to our church in Buckinghamshire called Don. He was a bit of a rough diamond, but he came to Christ and a few weeks later, he said to me, David should a Christian go to the cinema on Sunday evenings? Well now, I was tempted to quote Hezekiah 3:16 which, as you know, says a Christian must not go to the cinema Sunday evenings, but anyway I resisted the temptation and I said, Don I'm not going to tell you. He said, why not? I said, because you've got to find out from Jesus. Now if there had been something clear in scripture, I *would* have told him, because you can speak with authority where the Spirit has already spoken, but as far as I know, the Bible doesn't deal with that question so I said you must find out from Jesus. He said, well how do I find out? I said, take him with you next Sunday night and see if he enjoys the film. So the next Sunday night, Don goes to the local cinema in Gerrard's Cross there and he said to the girl in the box office, two tickets please. And he was all alone at the moment you see, nobody was standing with him. So the girl said, is your girlfriend joining you? He said, no that's alright, there's the money, give me two tickets. But she said, there's nobody with you. Look he said, let's not argue; there's the money, two tickets please. Well now her feminine curiosity just was not satisfied, and she said, well who's the other ticket for? And he said, well if you must know, it's for Jesus - and she got scared stiff. She lifted the telephone and asked the Manager to come down from his office. So the Manager came down; he said, what's the problem? Well he wants two tickets. Well give him two tickets - what did you call me down for? He wants one for Jesus, she said. And now the Manager couldn't handle it and he stuttered and he stammered and he said, well I suppose, you know, if he's willing to pay give him two tickets, you see - good business for us. So he got the two tickets and went inside. He said, you sit there Jesus; I'll sit here. And ten minutes into the film he said, are you enjoying it? And two minutes later he came out.

Now you see, there are some people who say that's bad shepherding. You should have taken responsibility for his decision. I believe it was good shepherding, you see? Because that's the liberty of the Spirit. It would be so easy for me to make a new rule. And I'm *not* saying it's wrong for a Christian to go to the cinema, but for *him* Jesus said 'not for *you*.' You see? Now this is the liberty of the Spirit, it's not doing what you want, and it's not doing what others tell you, it's letting the Spirit guide you. See, the real freedom, as Paul says in this letter, is not the freedom to sin, but it's the freedom *not to*. And that's real freedom, no unbeliever has that freedom, that's the freedom that God wants for us. But it's so easy to try and stop people going into the flesh by putting them under law. That's the only answer some fellowships have. Do you see? They're *trying* to protect their members from doing this and getting into that swamp without realising that that's just as bad as the cage, and legalism is just as much an enemy of liberty as license.

Now have you followed that? That's the whole argument of Galatians and chapters 1 and 2 talk about this liberty, chapters 3 and 4 talk about the legalism that can spoil it, chapters 5 and 6 talk about the opposite danger. So Paul is actually fighting on two fronts and that is the real problem, that on most issues you find yourself fighting on two fronts to keep the truth, to keep liberty - and walking that Striding Edge is really quite a delicate operation.

LEGALISM

So let's look at these three things. First of all, let's look a bit more closely at legalism. Circumcision is the first link in the chain for those Galatians. It would be the beginning of legalism - you *must* do this. And it is not part of the Gospel and they'd have to keep *all the rest*. But won't people take advantage when you tell them they're not under law, won't they become lawless? And one of the opposite errors is antinomianism, have you heard that word? Well you don't really *need* to know it, but 'anti' - against, nomianism – 'nomos' - law, it means that if you tell people they're not under law, won't they go and sin? And some people, you see, with their little minds can only see these two as the alternatives - that if you don't give them rules, they'll go and indulge themselves. Amazing how churches develop rules and regulations.

When I was a Methodist minister, there was a book half an inch thick called the Constitutional Practice and Discipline of the Methodist Church. It's now three and a quarter inches thick. There are 40 loose leaf pages added every year. Listen, if rules and regulations could bring revival, the Methodists would leave us standing. But it doesn't happen that way. How easy it is to try and regulate it and give rules for this, that and the other - and think that somehow our organisation will bring life. It doesn't. *Liberty* brings life and God set us free to *be free*. Watch legalism like a hawk. If you slip into it, you invariably become hard and hypocritical because you dare not tell other people if you're breaking the law, just daren't admit it in case you're thought to be unsound. Have you heard that word – legalism?

LICENSE

Let's look again at license. Yes, there is a real danger on this side and Paul says, the works of the flesh. Beware of them. There's a swamp, it's another form of slavery, it's sticky, sucking filth; it's easy to slide into it and very hard to get out of. And the works - plural notice - the works of the flesh, some are pretty crude - promiscuity, occultism, drugs, healists – there's a modern ring to all this; and then there are the subtle ones: quarrelling, rivalry, jealousy, envy, prejudice. Now those are pretty subtle ones but that's the swamp of the flesh. Now notice that here's Paul arguing like mad about circumcision, but he's talking about those who are just disagreeable either way, whatever issue is under discussion, who are constantly dividing people into parties and groups. That's another thing - you know what Paul is talking about I'm sure, this divisiveness, this awkwardness, the kind of personality that has so many corners you can't get near them. The kind of person who has faith to move mountains but leaves them in everybody else's path. Do you know the kind of person? I'm afraid there are one or two in every fellowship. It's of the flesh, it's subtle, but it's works of the flesh.

Now what happens, says Paul, when somebody slips into this swamp, and I'm afraid it's constantly happening, when there's some scandal in your fellowship, some scandal about a televangelist, what should the others do? And Paul, in a most solemn statement, he says if it's *occasional*, if they've just slipped into it, then pick them up quickly, because *you* might have slipped. There are a lot of banana skins on the Christian road. He said, if someone has *slipped* into sin, the rest of you get around and pick him up - and be humble as you do so because it might be you. But he says, *habitual* sin is quite a different matter. Someone who slips into the swamp, pick him up quickly, get them back in the fellowship, get them healed. But if someone deliberately and wilfully goes on wallowing in this then, he says, whatever a man sows, that will he also reap. And he's got a very solemn statement - if they go on in there, they will *not* inherit the Kingdom.

Now here again is a note I've sounded before which is one of the things that Christians are wrestling with today, this once-saved-always-saved thing, but listen to Paul. After listing the works of the flesh that go on in the swamp, he says, I warn you, as I've warned you before, those who *go on doing* these things will *never* inherit the Kingdom of God. Now he's talking to believers here, he's not talking about those who *slip* into it, and who need picking up quickly, but those who wallow in it and *go on*. They say, I'm alright I've got my ticket to heaven. And Paul says, you're not alright, you *won't* inherit the Kingdom. Now that's just one of his warnings and it's a very serious one.

You can slip into legalism, you can slip into license, and you need to be pulled quickly out of both. But if you deliberately and wilfully choose to *live there*, either in the cage or the swamp, then you don't inherit the Kingdom. And that's a serious warning we all need to hear.

TRUE LIBERTY

But now let's look at the liberty, which is the beautiful side of it all - the freedom *not to sin*. Isn't that a lovely freedom? You are free now, in Christ, not to sin. You don't need to say *yes*. As Paul puts it in, I think, his letter to Titus he said, we have been given the grace to say *no*. Which somebody else said is the finest contraceptive for the unmarried that they've ever come across. Given the grace to say no. You're free to say no. Isn't that beautiful?

THE FRUIT OF THE SPIRIT

Right. Well, let's now look what happens. Up on the ridge, though I couldn't put it on the diagram, there's a path along the top and we need to keep moving, as I've said earlier, we need to *walk* in the Spirit, and as you walk in the Spirit something beautiful happens. Fruit grows in your life. You *cannot* produce the fruit of the Spirit. You *can* produce the works of the flesh, but you can't produce the fruit of the Spirit, but as you keep walking along that Striding Edge, the fruit grows in your life. And there is only one fruit with nine flavours, whereas there are many works of the flesh, there's only one fruit, singular. But it has nine flavours. Now there is such a fruit in Spain and in the Mediterranean. It's called Monstera Deliciosa. You take a bite and it tastes like an orange and you take another bite and it tastes like a lemon and it has got all different flavours in it, Monstera Deliciosa, what a wonderful name for that fruit. When I'm speaking in a meeting I am always glad when someone has eaten it, as they can verify the truth of what I am saying about it. You'll have to take my word for it. I don't want you to think it is a preacher's story, you know? Daddy was that story true or were you just preaching, said a little boy. Terrible.

So the fruit of the Spirit, nine flavours. And all the flavours grow together; that's how you tell the fruit of the Spirit. You see, some of those flavours you *do* see in unbelievers, don't you? Some unbelievers have joy, others have peace, but you'll never see all nine together except in Christ and those filled with his Spirit and walking in his Spirit. You might see three or four in a good unbeliever but all nine growing together is proof that the Spirit is in that person's life and that they're walking in the Spirit. And the nine flavours relate you to God, other people and yourself. Three of those flavours, love, joy and peace, bring you into perfect harmony with God. The next three, patience, kindness and goodness, bring you into right harmony with other people. And then faithfulness, meekness and self-control bring you into a good relationship with yourself. What a lovely fruit they are.

Now then, the fruit are limited of course without the gifts of the Spirit, as the gifts are inadequate without the fruit. You know, if I went to hospital to visit a sick person I could show them all the fruit of the Spirit. I could show them love by visiting them and joy by cheering them up and peace by calming them down; patience, by listening to all the details of their operation; kindness, by giving them a bunch of grapes; goodness, by offering to look after the children; faithfulness by visiting them every day; meekness by leaving when the nurse tells me and self-control by not eating the grapes. Now, you see, I have demonstrated all the fruit of the Spirit in that visit, but I haven't healed them because that's a *gift* of the Spirit and we need both the gifts and the fruit. Never put these against each other.

But Paul says as you walk in the Spirit, the fruit grow and he uses the word *walk* here in two different ways, in fact, two different words. Unfortunately again, your English translation probably has *walk* both times. At the end of chapter 5, it says walk in the Spirit and in chapter 6 it says walk in the Spirit. In the Greek, chapter 5, walk is *peripatetic walking*, walkabout, what the Australians talk about - walkabout. It means to go for a walk by yourself like an Aborigine, but in chapter 6 the word walk is *march* in the Spirit - in step with others. Interesting! There are two kinds of walking in the Spirit. There's walk in the Spirit when we're by ourselves, and there's walking in step with the rest of our Christian brothers and sisters - and we need both. True liberty is walking along that height in step with your brothers and sisters. Walking in the Spirit together.

So that's the message of Paul's letter to the Galatians and I think it's one of the most *relevant* letters. It's not the most comfortable letter, but I would share the opinion of those who say this letter is the Magna Carta of Christian liberty. I really believe that's a wonderful title for it. If you want to know where we stand for freedom, this is our freedom. An awful lot of people are standing for *other* kinds of freedom, good or bad, but the freedom we stand for is the freedom not to sin. The freedom, the liberty of the Spirit, to keep out of that cage called legalism and out of that swamp called license, and keep up there on the heights enjoying the sunshine of God's favour.

Why is this so relevant? Well, sadly legalism is still with us. It's all over the place - people trying to get to heaven by their own works. Or even, having started in faith, going back to works, which is tragic. The late Dr W.E. Sangster went to visit a woman in hospital who was dying and he said to her, Are you ready to meet God, what will you say when you meet God? She held up worn hands; she said, I'm a widow, I've brought up five children, I've had no time for church or Bible or anything religious, but, she said, I've done the best for my children and when I see God I'll just hold up these hands and he'll look at these hands and he'll understand. Now what would you have said to a woman like that? Well Dr Sangster was a great Christian preacher, even preaching to one, and he just said to her, you're too late dear, you're too late. She said, what do you mean? Well, he said, there's somebody got in in front of you and he's holding up *his* hands in front of God - and God has eyes for no other. She said, what do you mean? And he was able to tell her, don't put your trust in *your* hands, put your trust in *his* hands.

LIBERTY - FREEDOM NOT TO SIN

You see, legalism is still with us, it's rife. The average Britisher thinks being a Christian is being kind to grandmother and the cat. You know the kind of thing? That's what they think, I am as good a Christian as anybody who goes to church. When they say that, they're right into legalism, and we've got to tell them that only 100% is good enough for heaven, and if you go there like you are now, you're going to ruin it for everybody else.

In churches too, churches are so prone to add their own rules to their membership. I teach four steps up to the front door, Repent, Believe, Be Baptised and Receive the Holy Spirit. There should be no more steps to the front door of the church, nothing more. The staircase is *inside*. There are a lot of other stairs to climb up inside as I bring out in 1 Peter, or 2 Peter, but there are only four steps outside. But unfortunately, we have the spectacle of churches who say you've got to be confirmed by a bishop or you've got to be this, or you've got to be that, you've got to be committed, you've got to accept the leadership, and all sorts of commitment is being added to the steps *outside* the household of God. Those steps come inside, and we should add no more than the scripture to the door of the household of God or we're into legalism.

And alas, license is still with us. There are still those who think that adultery by an unbeliever will take them to hell but adultery by a believer is okay. There are still those who believe this and who believe that sin in believers is somehow excused. You may lose a bit of blessing or you may lose a bit of reward, but you can't lose your ticket to heaven. Galatians deals with that very firmly and says, you don't inherit the Kingdom of God if you *deliberately* go back to this. You stay up on the height and you walk with others along Striding Edge, the wind of the Spirit blowing in your face and the sunshine of God's grace upon you, and you make it.

Well now. I think I'd better give you a bit of my translation of Galatians. It's such an exciting book. But listen to Paul's pleading:

> *"My brothers I beg you, please stand with me. After all, I was willing to identify with you; you've never hurt me before. You know it was because of physical illness that I first came to tell you the good news. My condition must have been a real trial to you, but you never made fun of it, nor were you even disgusted with me. Indeed, you gave me a welcome fit for a heavenly messenger or even the Messiah Jesus himself. You were so pleased and proud to have me. Where have all those feelings gone? I recall vividly that you wished it was possible to donate your eyes for transplanting in me. Now you seem to suspect me of being your enemy. Is that because I have been so honest with you? I know that these others are keen to make a fuss of you, but their motives are not good. They want to have you all to themselves so that you will make a fuss of them. Don't get me wrong, special attention is always fine, provided the intentions are right. You are my special concern even when I am not actually with you. My own children, I feel like a mother struggling with the pains of childbirth until Christ is brought right out in your lives. I just wish I could be with you at this moment so that you could hear the change in my tone of voice. I really am at my wit's end to know what to do about you."*

You feel the heart of Paul there? What an appeal that is.

> *"So my brothers, God meant you to be free. On the other hand, don't make this freedom an excuse for*

> *indulging your old self. Use it to show your love for others by putting yourselves at their service, for the whole Law can be expressed in just one principle, namely you are to care for your fellow man as much as you do about yourself, but if you snap at each other and pull each other to pieces, watch out that you don't end up by exterminating each other altogether. The approach I am advocating is to let God's Spirit decide each step you take. Then you just won't try to satisfy the desires of your old self, whose cravings are diametrically opposed to what God's Spirit wants and vice versa. The two are incompatible, which is why you find you can't always do what you really want to. If the Spirit is leading your life, you have nothing to fear from the Law."*

He finishes the letter:

> *"Don't be under any illusions, no-one can turn up their nose at God and get away with it. It is a universal law that a man must reap exactly what he has been sowing. If he cultivates his old self, he will harvest a character that has gone rotten. If he cultivates God's Spirit, that Spirit will produce a life of lasting quality. So let us never get fed up with doing good. One day there will be a grand harvest if we don't give up, so whenever we get the chance, let us give as much help as we can to everybody and especially to our immediate family of fellow believers. Look what sprawling letters I use in my own handwriting. It is those who are concerned about outward appearance and like to show off who are pressurising you into being circumcised. Their real object is to avoid the unpopularity associated*

with the cross of Jesus. Even though they observe circumcision, they don't seem to bother much about the rest of the Jewish law. They only want to get you circumcised so that they can brag about the number of converts to their ritual. Never let me boast about anything or anybody except the cross of Jesus. Through that execution I am now dead to society, and society is dead to me. Our standing in Christ is neither helped by being circumcised, nor hindered by remaining uncircumcised. What really matters is being made into a new person inside. All who live by this simple principle will receive the undisturbed harmony and undeserved help of God as will the true Israel. From now on, let no-one interfere with my work again. I have the marks I want on my body. I am branded with scars, gained in the service of Jesus. May the love of Jesus our divine Master and anointed Saviour fill your inmost being my brothers. So be it."

That's just a bit of the letter. One of the most powerful letters you will ever read. Try and read it in a modern translation as well. God bless you.

ABOUT DAVID PAWSON

A speaker and author with uncompromising faithfulness to the Holy Scriptures, David brings clarity and a message of urgency to Christians to uncover hidden treasures in God's Word.

Born in England in 1930, David began his career with a degree in Agriculture from Durham University. When God intervened and called him to become a Minister, he completed an MA in Theology at Cambridge University and served as a Chaplain in the Royal Air Force for three years. He moved on to pastor several churches, including the Millmead Centre in Guildford, which became a model for many UK church leaders. In 1979, the Lord led him into an international ministry. His current itinerant ministry is predominantly to church leaders. David and his wife Enid currently reside in the county of Hampshire in the UK.

Over the years, he has written a large number of books, booklets, and daily reading notes. His extensive and very accessible overviews of the books of the Bible have been published and recorded in *Unlocking the Bible*. Millions of copies of his teachings have been distributed in more than 120 countries, providing a solid biblical foundation.

He is reputed to be the "most influential Western preacher in China" through the broadcast of his best-selling *Unlocking the Bible* series into every Chinese province by Good TV. In the UK, David's teachings are often broadcast on Revelation TV.

Countless believers worldwide have also benefited from his generous decision in 2011 to make available his extensive audio video teaching library free of charge at www.davidpawson.org and we have recently uploaded all of David's video to a dedicated channel on www.youtube.com

BOOKS BY DAVID PAWSON
AVAILABLE FROM DAVIDPAWSON.COM

BIBLE COMMENTARIES

UNLOCKING THE BIBLE Omnibus ISBN 978 0 007166 66 4
UNLOCKING THE BIBLE - Charts, diagrams and images ISBN 978 1 911173 17 5

Introducing GENESIS ISBN 978 1 911173 80 9
Introducing The OLD TESTAMENT and HEBREW POETRY ISBN 978 1 911173 90 8

A Commentary on GENESIS Chapters 1-25 ISBN 978 1 911173 82 3
A Commentary on EXODUS ISBN 978 1 911173 85 4
A Commentary on Selected PSALMS ISBN 978 1 911173 91 5
A Commentary on ECCLESIASTES ISBN 978 1 911173 98 4
A Commentary on ISAIAH ISBN 978 1 913472 05 4
A Commentary on JEREMIAH ISBN 978 1 911173 76 2
A commentary on DANIEL ISBN 978 1 911173 06 9
A Commentary on THE MINOR PROPHETS ISBN 978 1 911173 94 6
A Commentary on ZECHARIAH ISBN 978 1 911173 38 0

A Commentary on the Gospel of MATTHEW ISBN 978 1 913472 09 2
A Commentary on the Gospel of MARK ISBN 978 1 909886 26 1
A Commentary on the Gospel of LUKE ISBN 978 1 911173 21 2
A Commentary on the Gospel of JOHN ISBN 978 1 909886 27 8
A Commentary on ACTS ISBN 978 1 909886 38 4
A Commentary on ROMANS ISBN 978 1 909886 78 0
A Commentary on 1 & 2 CORINTHIANS ISBN 978 1 909886 95 7
A Commentary on GALATIANS ISBN 978 1 909886 29 2
A Commentary on EPHESIANS ISBN 978 1 909886 98 8
A Commentary on PHILIPPIANS ISBN 978 1 909886 74 2
A Commentary on COLOSSIANS ISBN 978 1 913472 17 7
A Commentary on 1 & 2 THESSALONIANS ISBN 978 1 909886 73 5
A Commentary on 1 & 2 TIMOTHY, TITUS, PHILEMON - The Personal Letters ISBN 978 1 909886 70 4
A Commentary on HEBREWS ISBN 978 1 909886 33 9
A Commentary on JAMES ISBN 978 1 909886 72 8
A commentary on 1 & 2 PETER ISBN 978 1 909886 79 7
A Commentary on the LETTERS OF JOHN ISBN 978 1 909886 69 8
A Commentary on JUDE ISBN 978 1 909886 28 5
A Commentary on the book of REVELATION ISBN 978 1 909886 25 4

EXPLAINING SERIES
A CHRISTIAN DISCIPLESHIP PROGRAMME

THE AMAZING STORY OF JESUS ISBN 978 1 911173 29 8
THE RESURRECTION: The Heart of Christianity ISBN 978 1 911173 30 4
STUDYING THE BIBLE ISBN 978 1 911173 31 1
NEW TESTAMENT BAPTISM ISBN 978 1 911173 33 5
BEING ANOINTED AND FILLED WITH THE HOLY SPIRIT ISBN 978 1 911173 18 2
ETERNALLY SECURE? What the Bible says about being saved ISBN 978 1 911173 19 9
GRACE AND SALVATION: Generous, Undeserved, Co-Operation ISBN 978 1 911173 99 1
THE KEY STEPS TO BECOMING A CHRISTIAN ISBN 978 1 911173 87 8
THE TRINITY ISBN 978 1 911173 07 6
HOW TO STUDY A BOOK OF THE BIBLE: JUDE ISBN 978 1 911173 34 2
THE TRUTH ABOUT CHRISTMAS ISBN 978 1 911173 77 9
END TIMES ISBN 978 1 911173 46 5
WHAT THE BIBLE SAYS ABOUT WORK ISBN 978 1 911173 36 6
WHAT THE BIBLE SAYS ABOUT MONEY ISBN 978 1 911173 35 9
GRACE: Undeserved Favour, Irresistible Force or Unconditional Forgiveness?
ISBN 978 1 909886 84 1
THREE TEXTS OFTEN TAKEN OUT OF CONTEXT: Expounding the truth and exposing error
ISBN 978 1 909886 85 8
BUILDING A NEW TESTAMENT CHURCH ISBN 978 1 911173 69 4
DE-GREECING THE CHURCH: The impact of Greek thinking on Christian beliefs
ISBN 978 1 911173 20 5

TOPICAL BOOKS

Angels ISBN 978 1 909886 02 5
A Preacher's Legacy ISBN 978 1 911173 27 4
By God, I Will - The Biblical Covenants ISBN 978 1 909886 21 6
Christianity Explained ISBN 978 1 909886 64 3
Completing Luther's Reformation ISBN 978 1 911173 26 7
Defending Christian Zionism ISBN 978 1 909886 31 5
Heaven and Hell: A message of hope and warning to believers ISBN 978 1 913472 25 2
Is John 3:16 the Gospel? ISBN 978 1 909886 62 9
Israel in the New Testament (includes Galatians) ISBN 978 1 909886 57 5
Jesus Baptises In One Holy Spirit ISBN 978 1 909886 66 7
JESUS: The Seven Wonders of HIStory ISBN 978 1 909886 24 7
Kingdoms in Conflict ISBN 978 1 909886 04 9
Leadership Is Male ISBN 978 1 909886 67 4
Living in Hope ISBN 978 1 909886 65 0
Loose Leaves from My Bible ISBN 978 1 909886 55 1
Men for God ISBN 978 1 913472 20 7
Not As Bad As The Truth (David's Autobiography) ISBN 978 1 913472 35 1
Once Saved, Always Saved? ISBN 978 1 913472 27 6
Practising the Principles of Prayer ISBN 978 1 909886 63 6
Remarriage is Adultery Unless ... ISBN 978 1 909886 22 3
Simon Peter: The Reed and the Rock ISBN 978 1 909886 23 0
The Character of God ISBN 978 1 909886 34 6
The Challenge of Islam to Christians ISBN 978 1 913472 34 4
The God and the Gospel of Righteousness ISBN 978 1 909886 68 1
The Lord's Prayer ISBN 978 1 909886 71 1
The Maker's Instructions - A new look at the 10 Commandments
ISBN 978 1 909886 30 8
The Normal Christian Birth ISBN 978 1 913472 36 8
The Road To Hell ISBN 978 1 909886 59 9
Tributes by Friends of David Pawson ISBN 978 1 913472 21 4
Understanding the Resurrection ISBN 978 1 911173 22 9
Understanding the Second Coming ISBN 978 1 911173 23 6
Understanding Water Baptism ISBN 978 1 911173 24 3
What the Bible says about the Holy Spirit ISBN 978 1 909886 54 4
What I'm Looking Forward To: Life After Life After Death ISBN 978 1 913472 26 9
When Jesus Returns ISBN 978 1 913472 33 7
Where has the Body been for 2000 years? - Church history for beginners
ISBN 978 1 909886 20 9
Where is Jesus Now? ISBN 978 1 911173 78 6
Why Does God Allow Natural Disasters? ISBN 978 1 909886 58 2
Word And Spirit Together ISBN 978 1 909886 60 5

www.ingramcontent.com/pod-product-compliance
Lightning Source LLC
Chambersburg PA
CBHW071547080526
44588CB00011B/1820